Mum's Wonderful Cake

By Clem King

Eve and her brother Jack wanted to make a cake for their mother.

Mum started a new job on Monday, so tonight they would have a party to celebrate.

"What cake should we make?" asked Eve. "Honey cake?"

"Let's make a cake with some things Mum loves," said Jack. "Mum loves limes and dates."

"The only problem is, we don't have any limes," said Eve. "Or dates."

I'll ride Jack's bike to the shop and get some.
Take a bag and some money!

Dad got the limes and dates.

Just as he was about to pay, his phone rang.

"I wonder why Eve is calling," he said to himself.

Dad returned with dates, limes and a dozen eggs.

“Dad, the webpage says we need a cup of milk,” said Eve.
“But there is none in the fridge.”

I'll drive back to the shop.
I hope they don't need any other things.

Dad came home with milk.

“Pine nuts would be great to cover the cake’s sides!” said Eve.

"Do we have pine nuts?" asked Dad.

"No," Eve answered. "But that's all we need. Then we are done!"

Dad made another trip to the shop.

"Use this to mix the cake," Jack told Eve.

"And then the mix is done, right?" Eve said.

"There is nothing left to do but put it in the oven!"

Jack nodded.

Dad put on some gloves and put the cake in the oven to bake.

"Now we wait," he said.

Ding!

The oven timer went off.

"The cake is done!" said Eve.
"It smells wonderful!"

They waited for the cake to cool down.

"I'll cover the top with icing," Jack said.
"And add the pine nuts."

Pine
Nuts

A cake!
This is a wonderful surprise.
Thank you, kids!
Well done, Mum!
Well done, Mum!

CHECKING FOR MEANING

1. What did Dad have to get from the shop the first time he went? *(Literal)*
2. How did Dad get to the shop the second time? *(Literal)*
3. How do you think Mum felt when she saw the cake? *(Inferential)*
4. What kind of person is Dad? How do you know? *(Evaluative)*

EXTENDING VOCABULARY

limes	What do limes look like? How do they taste? What other foods are sour like limes?
dates	Dates are a type of food. How are dates used in the story? What other meanings can the word *dates* have?
dozen	How many items are there in a dozen? How many would you have if you had half a dozen?

MOVING BEYOND THE TEXT

1. A lime is a citrus fruit. What other citrus fruits have you tried?
2. If you were to bake a cake, what flavour cake would you make? What icing or decorations would you put on the top and sides?
3. What equipment is useful when you are baking?
4. The kids surprised Mum with a cake to celebrate her new job. What other occasions might you celebrate?

TIME TO WRITE

Imagine you are going to surprise someone. What do you plan to make for them? Who do you ask for help?